The 3rd Armada
Book of Fun

The 3rd Armada Book of Fun

Chosen by Mary Danby

Armada

The 3rd Armada Book of Fun was first published in the U.K.
in 1975 by William Collins Sons & Co. Ltd.,
14 St James's Place, London S.W.1.
Printed in Great Britain by Love & Malcomson Ltd.,
Brighton Road, Redhill Surrey.

Contents

Jokes, cartoons, limericks, puns, riddles,
verses, stories etc. and . . .

The line illustrations, where not otherwise acknowledged, are by Roger Smith, Marion Dickens, Esme Howard, Bernard Taylor and Jacquelyn Visick.

Acknowledgements

The Editor gratefully acknowledges permission to reprint copyright material to the following:

Messrs. Faber & Faber Ltd. for *My Sister Clarissa* by George Barker (from 'To Aylsham Fair') and *My Aunt* by Ted Hughes (from 'Meet My Folks'): Jonathan Clements for *Fun With Your Fish*, copyright © Jonathan Clements 1975; Spike Milligan and Dennis Dobson Publishers for *The Pig* and *What the Wiggle Woggle Said* (from 'A Book of Milliganimals'); Harry Hargreaves for the *Hayseeds* cartoons; George Harrap & Co. Ltd. and Little, Brown & Co. for the following verses by David McCord: *Mr. Bidery's Spidery Garden* (from 'Mr. Bidery's Spidery Garden', published by Harrap, and 'For Me to Say', published by Little, Brown, copyright © 1970 David McCord) and *Four Limericks* (from 'Mr Bidery's Spidery Garden' published by Harrap, and 'Write Me a Verse', published by Little, Brown, copyright © 1961 62 by David McCord); Bernard Taylor for *James and the Toaster*, copyright © Bernard Taylor 1975; David Higham Associates Ltd. for *Table of Grips and Tortures for Masters* (from 'Down With Skool') copyright © Geoffrey Willans and Ronald Searle; Kay Leith for *Pudding Head*, copyright © Kay Leith 1975; Mrs. E. V. Rieu for *The Flattered Flying-Fish* by E. V. Rieu; Gerald Duckworth & Co. Ltd for *The Elephant* by Hilaire Belloc (with drawings by BTB) (from 'The Bad Child's Book of Beasts'); the Estate of A. P. Herbert, and A. P. Watt & Son for *The Centipede*. *The Butler* by Archibald Marshal' (with drawings by George Morrow), (from 'Simple People') and *Etiquette for Animals*, are reproduced by permission of 'Punch'. Syndication International for *Our Friend Augustus, Professor Pi, Suky Sue* and cartoons on pages 14 16, 23, 30, 34, 43 54, 55, 63, 74 75, 83 94 103 113 and 114 Associated Newspapers for *Double Trouble, Fred Basset* and cartoons on pages 9, 11, 23 45, 54 63, 74 83 and 94. London Express News & Feature Services for *Clive* and *Penelope*.

Note:
Every effort has been made to trace the owners of the copyright material in this book. It is the Editor's belief that all necessary permissions have been obtained, but in the case of any question arising as to the use of any material, the Editor will be pleased to make the necessary correction in future editions of the book.

Have You Heard This One?

What happened to the plastic surgeon who fell asleep in front of the fire?
He melted.

Woman: I'd like a bar of soap please.
Chemist: Certainly. Would you like it scented?
Woman: No thank you. I'll take it with me now.

What did Dick Turpin say at the end of his ride?
'Whoa!'

Harry: I know a man called Arthur Smells. He wants to change his name.
Larry: I'm not surprised. What's he changing it to?
Harry: Fred Smells.

'If this one's Marge, I suppose the other one is Butter.'

Ted: Why do you call your wife Treasure?
Ned: Because people keep asking me where I dug her up.

Teacher: How do you spell 'crocodile'?
Pupil: K-r-o-k-o-d-i-a-l.
Teacher: The dictionary spells it c-r-o-c-o-d-i-l-e.
Pupil: You didn't ask me how the dictionary spelt it, you asked how *I* spelt it.

What happened to the snake with a cold?
She adder viper nose.

Judge: Why did you steal that purse?
Prisoner: I wasn't feeling well, Your Honour, and I thought the change might do me good.

Notice in a newspaper: Our statement last week that Mr. Sam Snoop was a defective in the police force was, of course, a misprint. Mr. Snoop is a detective in the police farce.

Pam: My teacher does bird imitations.
Sam: Really?
Pam: Yes. She watches me like a hawk.

The thing about fish fingers is that they're so handy.

Father: Why were you kept in after school today?
Son: I didn't know where the Orkneys were.
Father: Well, in the future, just remember where you put things.

10

Psychiatrist to patient: When did you get this feeling that nobody liked you, you ugly, boring, dreary, dislikeable little man?

A Russian named Rudolf looked out of a boarding-house window and announced: 'It's raining.'
'No it isn't,' said the landlady. 'That's sleet, not rain.'
Her husband shook his head.'You're wrong. Remember, Rudolf the Red knows rain, dear.'

Mother: Eat your cabbage, Jimmy. It'll put colour in your cheeks.
Jimmy: But I don't *want* green cheeks!

A little girl opened the door to her teacher.
'Are your parents in?' asked the teacher.
'They was in,' said the little girl, 'but they is out now.'
' "They was in", "they is out"!' exclaimed the teacher. 'Where's your grammar?'
'In the front room watching telly.'

'Here it is, m'lord—concrete evidence!'

11

My Sister Clarissa
by George Barker

My sister Clarissa spits twice if I kiss her
and once if I hold her hand.
I reprimand her—my name's Alexander—
for spitting I simply can't stand.

'Clarissa, Clarissa, my sister, is this a
really nice habit to practise?'
But she always replies with innocent eyes
rather softly, 'Dear Brother, the fact is

'I think I'm an ape with a very small grape
crushed to juice in my mastodon lips.
Since I am not a prude, though I hate being rude,
I am simply ejecting the pips.'

Limerick Laughs

To London there came, from Korea,
A man with a great big left ear,
  As a blanket, at night,
  It was valuable, quite,
But in a packed Tube train—oh, dear!

A thrifty young fellow of Shoreham
Made brown paper trousers and woreham;
  He looked nice and neat
  Till he bent in the street
To pick up a pin; then he toreham.

There was an old lady who said
When she found a thief under her bed,
  'Get up from the floor,
  You're too close to the door,
And I fear you'll take cold in the head.'

There was a young lady named Maggie,
Whose dog was enormous and shaggy;
  The front end of him
  Looked vicious and grim—
But the tail end was friendly and waggy.

'I'm not just a pretty face, y'know!'

'That horse has never won a photo-finish yet!'

'I've been evicted.'

A Bunch of Riddles

Why do white sheep eat more grass than black sheep?
Because there are more of them.

Do you need training to be a litter collector?
No, you just pick it up as you go along.

Why can't a steam engine sit down?
Because it has a tender behind.

What did the pilot say when he took off?
'Must fly now.'

What did the big telephone say to the little telephone?
'You're too young to be engaged.'

Why is the letter E lazy?
Because it is always in bed.

What does a ball do when it stops rolling?
It looks round.

Why does a bald-headed man have no use for keys?
Because he has lost his locks.

What's the difference between a mouldy lettuce and a
dismal song?
One's a bad salad and the other's a sad ballad.

On the Couch

Patient: I've got this strange feeling I'm a bell.
Psychiatrist: Well, if you're not better in a day or two, give me a ring.

Patient: Doctor, I keep losing my temper with people.
Psychiatrist: I see. Tell me about it.
Patient: I've just flipping well told you about it, you stupid old buffer!

Patient: I feel like a pair of curtains.
Psychiatrist: Well pull yourself together.

Patient: It's an odd thing, Doctor, but I keep dreaming about being covered in gold paint.
Psychiatrist: Ah-hah! You must have a gilt complex!

*'Don't worry about his loss of memory, Doctor.
It wasn't a very good one.'*

Penelope
by Thelwell

Nonsense Verse

As I was standing in the street,
As quiet as could be,
A great big ugly man came up
And tied his horse to me.

Get up, get up you lazy-head,
Get up, you lazy sinner.
We need those sheets for tablecloths—
It's nearly time for dinner!

Hickory, dickory dock,
Two mice ran up the clock;
The clock struck one—
But the other one got away.

Somebody said that it couldn't be done,
But he, with a grin, replied
He'd never be one to say it couldn't be done—
Leastways, not till he'd tried.
So he buckled right in, with a trace of a grin,
By golly, he went right to it.
He tackled The Thing That Couldn't Be Done!
And he couldn't do it.

Fun With Your Fish
by Jonathan Clements

If you want to keep the very latest thing in pets, you must bid a tearful farewell to your dog Snoopy and cat Sylvester—and shake hands with a fish. Or, rather, shake fins. For these days fish are all the rage. And not only with chips. Fish are kept, in underwater luxury, by some of the top people in the land.

Should you decide to adopt a fish for a pet, you'll have to give it a centrally-heated aquarium for a home. An old jam-jar or deep-sea diver's helmet just won't do.

The fish that people are so crazy about nowadays aren't the good old-fashioned goldfish. There are fancy Hindu bull-fish, Japanese butterfly-fish, Lithuanian toad-fish, Mexican killer-fish, and little fish from darkest Africa which grin wickedly at you through the glass.

If you *still* want to keep fish, you must bear in mind that they are extremely stupid. Fish have to be told everything at least twice. And in a nice voice, too. If you scold them, they're liable to sulk—then sink. And you mustn't expect anything in return for all your troubles. There is no pet in existence as ungrateful as a fish, I'm sorry to say.

But if you insist on taking up this foolish pastime, here are some valuable hints and tips regarding the welfare and upbringing of your fish.

19

ONE: The water that your fish swim in must be exactly the right temperature. A thermometer may be used—but it's better for you yourself to get into the aquarium first and test the temperature. If it's warm enough for you, it's warm enough for the fish.

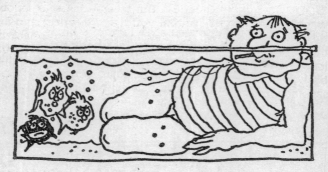

TWO: Let your fish watch lots of television. Have the aquarium facing the set at all times. Their favourite programmes include 'Blue Peter', 'Monty Python's Flying Circus' and almost any weather forecast.

THREE: Dump little objects into the aquarium for the fish to play with. (No, *not* your baby brother or sister!) Plastic crocodiles and dinosaurs, as well as toy machine guns and cutlasses, should look good on the sandy tank-bed. Even though they might well scare the wits out of the fish.

FOUR: To make the fish feel as if they're going somewhere, it's a good idea to paste pretty seaside postcards on the inside walls of the tank.

FIVE: Never give fish rich, starchy foods, for their little stomachs are very delicate. In fact, some of them have no stomachs at all—just heads and tails. Try them on a diet of worms and watercress, with lemon meringue pie for pudding.

SIX: Give your pet fish plenty of exercise. This can be done by going right up to the glass and staring at them. Making ugly faces at them (as they are at you), shout 'BOOOOO!' or 'WHEEEEE!'. But be sure to use a serious voice, so the fish realise that you mean business and are their master. They will then swim quickly to the back of the tank, and come back for more. If you keep this up for long enough, they will get quite a lot of exercise swimming back and forth, and you will get a certain amount of satisfaction as well.

SEVEN: If your fish aren't fit after all this, more drastic steps are called for. Take the whole aquarium— fish and all—out on horseback through open country. Fish love horseback-riding, if it's done with somebody they love and trust.

EIGHT: Before they go to sleep at night, be sure to tuck your fish up in their sand or seaweed, and sing them

a soothing lullaby. And whatever you do, don't forget to put on their waterproof pyjamas. (On the fish, not you!)

All of this sounds as if it's a lot of trouble to keep fish. Well, it is. One solution to the problem is simply not to keep any fish at all. Then at least you will have your time to yourself. And you can welcome back your dog Snoopy and cat Sylvester with open arms. At least they purr with happiness, and wag their tails to express the pleasure they take in your company.

'Oh—it's just a stage he's going through!'

'I've never met such a flippin' knowall!'

'He hasn't killed any bulls—but he holds the record for the fastest lap!'

The Pig
by Spike Milligan

A very rash young lady pig
(They say she was a smasher)
  Suddenly ran
  Under a van—
Now she's a gammon rasher.

Crazy Ads

For Sale: Saloon car, the property of an old lady in first-class condition.

Lost: Five-year-old girl, wearing a dress patterned with pink roses and yellow socks.

Bargain: Smooth-running hearse. Body needs attention.

Wanted: Electric drill suitable for boring rig operator.

Beauty Hint: Whipped Cream Face Masks. Apply to your milkman.

For Hire: Three-foot artificial leg.

Found: Two dozen bottles of whiskey. Apply to addresh at top of thish page.

Pet's Corner: If your cat cannot drink fresh milk you should boil it.

My Aunt
by Ted Hughes

You've heard how a green thumb
Makes flowers come
Quite without toil
Out of any old soil.

Well, my Aunt's thumbs were green.
At a touch, she had blooms
Of prize Chrysanthemums—
The grandest ever seen.

People from miles around
Came to see those flowers
And were truly astounded
By her unusual powers.

One day a little weed
Pushed up to drink and feed
Among the pampered flowers
At her water-can showers.

Day by day it grew
With ragged leaves and bristles
Till it was tall as me or you—
It was a King of Thistles.

'Prizes for flowers are easy,'
My Aunt said in her pride.
'But was there ever such a weed
The whole world wide?'

She watered it, she tended it,
It grew alarmingly.
As if I had offended it,
It bristled over me.

'Oh Aunt!' I cried. 'Beware of that!
I saw it eat a bird.'
She went on polishing its points
As if she hadn't heard.

'Oh Aunt!' I cried. 'It has a flower
Like a lion's beard——'
Too late! It was devouring her
Just as I had feared!

Her feet were waving in the air—
But I shall not proceed.
Here ends the story of my Aunt
And her ungrateful weed.

Hayseeds
by Hargreaves

MORNING, NOON AND NIGHT....

.. I GIVE MY TONGUE AN AIRING OUTSIDE ..

.. IT MUST BE AWFUL FOR IT TO STAY BUNCHED UP ALL DAY BEHIND MY TEETH!

Four Limericks
by David McCord

There once was a man on the Moon.
But he got there a little too soon.
   Some others came later
   And fell down a crater—
When *was* it? Next August? Last June?

Take the curious case of Tom Pettigrew
And Hetty, his sister. When Hettigrew
   As tall as a tree
   She came just to Tom's knee.
And did *Tom* keep on growing? You bettigrew.

I don't much exactly quite care
For these cats with short ears and long hair;
   But if anything's worse
   It's the very reverse:
Just you ask any mouse anywhere.

There was a young man, let me say,
Of West Pumpkinville, Maine, U.S.A.
   You tell me there's not
   Such a place? Thanks a lot.
I forget what he did anyway.

More Jokes

Did you hear about the electrician named Watt who was charged with battery? They put him a dry cell. It was a terrible shock.

Father to Son: How many trillions of times have I told you not to exaggerate?

What's the best thing to give as a parting gift?
A comb.

Patient: Will my measles be better in time for the party next week?
Doctor: Well, I hate to make rash promises . . .

Three rather deaf old ladies met in the street.
'Windy, isn't it?' said one.
'No, it's Thursday,' said the second.
'So am I,' said the third. 'Let's all go and have a cup of tea.'

'It's the mini-monk look!'

A Nautical Ballad
by Charles E. Caryl

A capital ship for an ocean trip
Was the *Walloping Window-blind*;
No gale that blew dismayed her crew,
Nor troubled the captain's mind.

The man at the wheel was taught to feel
Contempt for the wildest blow;
And it often appeared—when the weather had cleared—
He had been in his bunk below.

The boatswain's mate was very sedate,
Yet fond of amusement, too;
And he played hopscotch with the starboard watch,
While the captain tickled the crew.

A NAUTICAL BALLAD

And the gunner we had was apparently mad,
For he sat on the after-rail
And fired salutes with the captain's boots
In the teeth of the booming gale.

The captain sat on the commodore's hat
And dined, in a royal way,
Off toasted pigs and pickles and figs
And gunnery bread each day.

The cook was Dutch and behaved as such,
For the diet he gave the crew
Was a number of tons of hot cross buns,
Served up with sugar and glue.

A NAUTICAL BALLAD

All nautical pride we laid aside,
And we cast our vessel ashore
On the Gulliby Isles, where the Poo-poo smiles
And the Rumpletum-bunders roar.

We sat on the edge of a sandy ledge,
And shot at the whistling bee:
And the cinnamon bats wore waterproof hats
As they danced by the sounding sea.

On Rug-gub Bark, from dawn till dark
We fed, till we all had grown
Uncommonly shrunk—when a Chinese junk
Came in from the Torriby Zone.

She was stubby and square, but we didn't much care,
So we cheerily put to sea;
And we left the crew of the junk to chew
The bark of the Rug-gub tree.

Seaside Fun

'Welcome to sunny Brightsea—
and please don't leave wet
umbrellas, raincoats and galoshes
in the bedroom.'

'... and it's only a few
minutes from the sea.'

'Well, at least we'll be able to go
straight in swimming after THIS lunch!'

Punorama

Armageddon: ARMAGEDDON outer here

Beret: BERET the hatchet

Cashmere: Can you CASHMERE cheque?

Dismal: Britain now has DISMAL currency

Eyesore: EYESORE what you did

Fuel: Don't be a silly FUEL

Ginger: GINGER yourself when you fell down?

Hence: Wash your face and HENCE

Immigrate: She gave IMMIGRATE big kiss

Juno: JUNO why she did it?

Kipper: We'll KIPPER welcome in the hillsides

Lettuce: LETTUCE pray

Morphia: You get MORPHIA money here

Neurosis: We planted some NEUROSIS in the garden

Offal: I have some OFFAL news for you

Palmist: PALMIST the train

Quarter: They QUARTER stealing apples

Rodent: This RODENT wide enough

Schedule: In the SCHEDULE find an axe

Tweak: Come back next TWEAK

Unit: UNIT while I crochet

Vicious: There are VICIOUS in the sea

Wafer: Make WAFER the procession

Xenon: We'll see you XENON Sunday

Yoga: YOGA your way, I'll go mine

Z: So I Z to him, I Z.

Suky Sue
by Roger Mahoney

More Riddles

What is the person called who puts you in touch with the spirit world?
A bartender.

What are hippies for?
To hang your leggies from.

What is the best way to make a fire from two sticks?
Make sure one of the sticks is a match.

What dog has no tail?
A hot dog.

What is the difference between a stupid Dutchman and a drainpipe?
One is a silly Hollander and the other is a hollow cylinder.

Why did the teacher wear dark glasses?
Because the class was so bright.

Why did the apple turnover?
Because it saw the banana split.

What is the difference between a cloud and a boy being spanked?
One pours with rain and the other roars with pain.

What should you do if you see a big tiger?
Hope that the tiger doesn't see you.

Zoo Talk

'EWE GNU here, DEER?'

'Yes. KUDU help me? I MUSQUASH my hands, but some BEASTly CHEETAH is HOGging the BISON.'

'For heaven's SNAKES, what a BOAR! Find the CHIMPANZEE if he can aLLAMA, for RHINO I've ADDER-nough of her MONKEY tricks. Now I must GOAT to bed and get some SHEEP. The sun's getting OTTER—it's a real GORILLA—and we should be LION down as we've some AARDVARK to do later. Anyway, this YAKking makes me HORSE.'

Etiquette for Animals

Should a cassowary curtsey to a camel?
Should a porpoise say 'Good morning' to a shark?
Should a salamander bow to a solitary cow?
If he meets her in the village after dark?

Should barnacles wear billycocks or bowlers?
Should centipedes wear Wellingtons, or what?
If a lobster's out to tea, and he's got a cold, should he
Be allowed to keep his muffler on or not?

Should rhinoceroses bathe in public places?
Is a porcupine at parties quite the thing?
If a llama comes to call and he hasn't washed at all,
Does it matter if one doesn't hear him ring?

Should a dolphin dilly-dally with a dogfish?
Should a caterpillar parley with a snail?
If a guinea-pig should talk with a squirrel as they walk,
Should the squirrel raise the topic of a tail?

Should hyenas laugh at things that are not funny?
Say, an antelope eloping with an elk?
Should storks go in for stilts and should grouse adopt the
   kilts?
May a winkle pull a cracker with a whelk?

Epitaphs

Here lies what's left
Of Leslie More.
No Les.
No more.

Beneath this stone and lump of clay
Lies Uncle Peter Daniels,
Who too early in the month of May
Took off his winter flannels.

Here lies the body of Jonathan Pound,
Who was lost at sea and never found.
Drowned, drowned, against his wishes,
Down, down, among the fishes.

On Charles II
Here lies our Sovereign Lord the King,
Whose word no man relies on,
Who never said a foolish thing,
Nor ever did a wise one.

John Wilmot, Earl of Rochester

Mischief-Makers

'Two thousand, three hundred
and four pieces of coal.'

'Other boys collect train
numbers . . . make models . . .'

'Don't shout so loud,
Mum, you'll wake the
baby-sitter.'

Oldies

One day I went out to the Zoo,
For I wanted to see the old Gnu,
But the old Gnu was dead
And the new Gnu they said
Was too new a new Gnu to view.

There was an old man of St. Bees,
Who was stung on the arm by a wasp.
When asked, 'Does it hurt?'
He replied, 'No, it doesn't,
I'm so glad it wasn't a hornet.'

W. S. Gilbert

There was an old man of Toronto,
And people said: 'Where has he gone to?
Here's his table and chair,
But where is he, where,
This invisible man of Toronto?'

Andrew Lang

There was a young maid who said, 'Why
Can't I look in my ear with my eye?
If I give my mind to it,
I'm sure I can do it.
You never can tell till you try.'

Witty Waiters

Diner: I say, waiter! There's a twig in my soup.
Waiter: Hang on, sir—I'll call the branch manager.

Diner: A cup of coffee without cream, please.
Waiter: We haven't any cream, sir. Will you take it without milk?

Diner: This lobster has only got one claw.
Waiter: Well, maybe it was in a fight, sir.
Diner: Well, maybe you could bring me the winner.

Diner: What's wrong with these eggs?
Waiter: Don't ask me, sir; I only laid the table.

Diner: I don't like this cheese.
Waiter: But it's Gruyere, sir.
Diner: Well, bring me some that grew somewhere else.

'Waiter—there's a hair-piece in my soup.'

Library Laughs

'A Nurse's Life' by Ann T. Septic

'Crossword Puzzles' by Ivor Clue

'The Last Sandwich' by Arthur Anymore

'Carpet Buying' by Walter Wall

'Central Heating' by Ray D. Ator

'Au Revoir' by C. U. Later

'Neigh! Neigh!' by G. Gees

'The Wobbly Ladder' by Hugo First

'Greengrocer's Pride' by Joyce Cabbages

'Old Furniture' by Ann Teak

'What the Butler Saw' by Mustapha Nutherlook

'He's Ready' by Dennis E. Cumming

'No Through Road' by Ron Turning

'The Great White Bird' by Al B. Tross

'Splitting the Atom' by Molly Cule

'Loud Rumblings' by M. T. Tumm

'You Must Be Joe King' by Paul D. Utherwun

'Hark to the Singing!' by Harold Angels

'Order in School' by Emma Prefect

'The Eagle's Talons' by Claude Feet

'One Card Short' by Delia Another

'The North Wind' by Gail Force

'Sitting on a Leaf' by Harry Caterpillar

'Bang! Bang!' by Tommy Gunn

'High Spirits' by Duncan Disorderly

'Short Measure' by Milly Metre

'Making Merry' by Hans Neesanboompsadaisy

Clive
by Angus McGill

James and the Toaster
by Bernard Taylor

A brand-new toaster gave to James
A promise of exciting games.
He'd SNAP the bread into the slot
And watch while all the bars grew hot.
With smiles of glee and eyes so bright
He'd watch the shining little light
While waiting till the toast was done . . .
And then he'd SNAP it out. What fun!
His mother said, 'You foolish boy!
It isn't meant to be a toy!'
But on he went, that foolish James,
Intent upon his little games,
Till—somewhat bored with toasting bread—
He searched for something else instead;

JAMES AND THE TOASTER

And, as his mother turned to look,
She saw him toast a picture-book.

And later, when her back was turned,
Her new blue Sunday hat got burned.

Cakes and cushions, legs of lamb,
Rugs and carpet, beef and ham:
Everything went up in flames;
Nothing was safe from naughty James.
His mother said, 'It's just no joke
To have my kitchen filled with smoke.'
While Father smacked him hard and said:
'Straight upstairs and into bed!
And there you'll stay until you've learnt
That certain things must NOT be burnt.'

So naughty James went off to sleep
With not a single crumb to eat.

At breakfast, James said: 'As I'm told,
I will remain as good as gold.
From now on,' he proudly boasted,
'Not one thing shall you find toasted.'

'Good boy!' his mother said to him,
And gently kissed our little Jim.
'Eat up your wholesome wholemeal bread
While I go up and make your bed.'

But, oh, the moment she was gone,
He found the toaster lure was on,

JAMES AND THE TOASTER

And, just to pay his father back,
He took his Dad's new cricket bat,
Then, leaping light as he was able,
Jumped upon the breakfast table . . .

Oh, silly James, he should have known
To leave forbidden things alone;
For, hot upon his escapade,
He stepped into the marmalade,
And, skidding to a sudden stop,
He fell into the toaster—PLOP!

Later, when his mum came down,
She found him crisp—and golden-brown.

Daft Riddles

What goes 'ha, ha, ha, plop!'?
Someone laughing his head off.

What's yellow and white and travels at 90 m.p.h.?
An engine driver's egg sandwiches.

What's white and goes up?
A stupid snowflake.

What's round and bad-tempered?
A vicious circle.

What's yellow on the inside and green on the outside?
A banana disguised as a cucumber.

What goes 'hic! hic! hic!'?
A cracked record of 'Hickory Dickory Dock'.

What walks backwards through walls going 'Er, boo!'?
A nervous ghost.

What goes 'How d'you do? How d'you do? How d'you
do? How d'you do? How d'you do? How d'you do?
How d'you do?'?
An octopus with a broken arm.

'When's blast-off time?'

'I'm bored. Let's try
on some hats.'

'See what I mean?'

What's the Trouble?

Jessie: I keep seeing little black spots before my eyes.
Tessie: Have you seen a doctor?
Jessie: No, only little black spots.

Patient: Doctor, I'm having trouble with my breathing.
Doctor: Well, I'm sure I can give you something to stop that.

The doctor told Henry he could get rid of his cold by drinking some medicine after a hot bath, but the bath water went cold before Henry could drink it all.

Patient: Doctor, I get a stabbing pain in my eye every time I drink a cup of tea.
Doctor: Have you tried taking the spoon out?

In hospitals, what is taken but never missed?
Your temperature

'Hello? Pardon? Speak up!'

Limerick Time

There was an old man of Bombay,
Who stood on his head all the day
   In the main thoroughfare,
   With his legs in the air,
Begging for alms by the way.

Whenever a matron named Frances
Goes to big hospital dances,
   She carries some lint,
   Several pins and a splint,
Explaining, 'I never take chances.'

An optimist living at Datchet
Attempted to shave with a hatchet.
   When his nose he did sever,
   He said, 'Now I'll never
Have nasal catarrh—I can't catch it."

A sleeper from the Amazon
Put nighties of his gra'mazon—
   The reason that
   He was too fat
To get his own pyjamazon.

Fred Basset
by Graham

A Quadrupedremian Song
by Tom Hood

He dreamt that he saw the Buffalant,
And the spottified Dromedaraffe,
The blue Camelotamus, lean and gaunt,
And the wild Tigeroceros calf.

The maned Liodillo loudly roared,
And the Peccarbok whistled its whine,
The Chinchayak leapt on the dewy sward,
As it hunted the pale Baboopine.

He dreamt that he met the Crocoghau,
As it swam in the Stagnolent Lake;
But everything that in dreams he saw
Came of eating too freely of cake.

Four Funnies

Brown has a lovely baby girl,
The stork left her with a flutter;
Brown he named her Margarine,
For he hadn't any but her.

The Queen of Hearts was making tarts
In a great big china basin;
Alas! Alack! She turned her back,
And a poodle dipped his face in.

Women's faults are many,
But men have only two:
Everything they say,
And everything they do.

Jerry Hall
Is so small
A rat could eat him
Hat and all.

Table of Grips and Tortures for Masters from 'Down With Skool'

by Geoffrey Willans and Ronald Searle

The plain blip for numskulls

Side hair tweak exquisitely painful

Single-hair extraction for non-attenders

The cork in the storm for violent temperaments

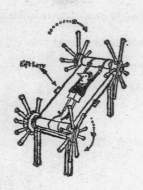

Portable rack for maths masters (with thumbscrew attachment)

The headshave with ruler

The Cumberland creep from behind with silver pencil

The simple open furnace

Person to Person

1st Cannibal: I don't know what to make of my husband these days.
2nd Cannibal: How about a hot-pot?

Jenny: Does your watch tell the time?
Penny: No, you have to look at it.

Dan: Do you like your job, cleaning chimneys?
Stan: Soots me!

Old Lady: Must I stick this stamp on myself?
Post Office Clerk: No, stick it on the envelope.

1st Boy Scout: I failed my first-aid test today.
2nd Boy Scout: Why was that?
1st Boy Scout: I tried to bandage a hiccup.

Mother: Well, Johnny, do you think that your teacher likes you?
Johnny: Oh yes. She puts a big kiss by all my sums.

Girl: Care to join me?
Boy: Why, are you coming apart?

Molly: I've just bought a wig. Shall I tell my boyfriend?
Polly: No, I should keep it under my hat if I were you.

Outer Space

'I'll let my Bobby out to play with you WHEN he's done his homework!'

'Take me to your leader—and take your finger out of your ear when you speak to an officer.'

"Next week, I'll sell you another casket of earth treasure!"

The Cruel Naughty Boy

There was a cruel naughty boy
Who sat upon the shore,
A-catching little fishes by
The dozen and the score.

And as they squirmed and wriggled there,
He shouted loud with glee,
'You surely cannot want to live,
You're little-er than me.'

Just then with a malicious leer,
And a capacious smile,
Before him from the water deep
There rose a crocodile.

He eyed the little naughty boy,
Then heaved a blubbering sigh,
And said, 'You cannot want to live,
You're little-er than I.'

The fishes squirm and wriggle still,
Beside that sandy shore;
The cruel little naughty boy
Was never heard of more.

More Rhymes

Little Willie, mean as hell,
Pushed his sister in the well;
Mother said, while drawing water,
'My, it's hard to raise a daughter!'

Don't worry if your job is small
And your rewards are few;
Remember that the mighty oak
Was once a nut like you!

...ed on the burning deck,

Limericks by Edward Lear

There was an Old Man who said, 'Hush!
I perceive a young bird in this bush!'
   When they said—'Is it small?'
   He replied—'Not at all!

The boy stood
Eating peanuts by the peck;
His father called him, he wouldn't go
Because he loved the peanuts so.

If a man who turnips cries
Cry not when his father dies,
It is proof that he would rather
Have a turnip than his father.

Samuel Johnson (1786)

A toast:
Here's champagne to our real friends,
And real pain to our sham friends.

c

There was a young lady in blue,
Who said, 'Is it you? Is it you?'
   When they said, 'Yes, it is,'
   She replied only, 'Whizz!'
That ungracious young lady in blue.

There was an Old Man who said, 'Well!
Will *nobody* answer this bell?
    I have pulled day and night,
    Till my hair has grown white,
But nobody answers this bell!'

There was an Old Man in a boat,
Who said, 'I'm afloat! I'm afloat!'
    When they said, 'No! you ain't!'
    He was ready to faint,
That unhappy Old Man in a boat.

Professor Pi
by Bob van den Born

Pudding Head
by Kay Leith

Mr. Bun was about to close the shop for the night when a man came in and looked around. As soon as he opened his mouth, Mr. Bun realised that he was a foreigner of some kind.

'Appundabattashots,' the man said.

Mr. Bun looked quickly at his shelves, as if he didn't know already exactly what was there: chocolate, boiled sweets, crystallised fruits, peppermints—and in the freezer were iced lollies, blocks of ice-cream of all kinds. You think of it, Mr. Bun had it. But nothing that sounded remotely like Appundabattashots. It sounded like something you put in a gun.

'Appunda . . . ?'

The man nodded his head. 'I weesh Appundabattashots.'

Mr. Bun thought rapidly. 'Bitter lemon?' He held up a bottle of you-know-what.

'No, no. Appundabattashots.'

One by one, Mr. Bun held up the bars of chocolate so temptingly laid out on the counter. Each time the man shook his head, becoming increasingly impatient and annoyed.

'What do you do with it?' asked Mr. Bun.

The man pointed to his mouth. 'I eat.'

Mrs. Bun, at home ten minutes' walk away, was about to serve dinner, but her husband was not going to be beaten by this thing. 'Point to it, then,' he prompted.

'I no see eet.'

'Well, look around.'

The man seemed doubtful.

'Go on—have a look. Do you think you'll know it when you see it?'

The man's smile was pitying. 'Oh, yes. I know.'

69

Both men moved around, staring at boxes and jars and peering inside the freezer.

'Who makes this Appundabattashots?'

The foreigner thought for a moment. 'Ees made by mens in Laddeeskeert.'

Mr. Bun had never heard of that place. 'Pontefract cakes?'

'What ees thees Pondefrackakes?'

Fifteen minutes went by, and if for nothing else but curiosity the shopkeeper was determined to find out what this strange substance was. 'Is it sweet?'

'Ees sweet, yes.'

'Is it crunchy?'

'Crunchee?'

'Oh, never mind.'

Half an hour went by.

'I theenk I go,' said the man, edging to the door.

'Oh, no, please!' begged Mr. Bun. Imagine going through life not knowing what Appundabattashots was!

'Come into the back shop. Let's look round in there.'

The man backed away and Mr. Bun snatched at his arm. 'Please!'

The foreigner looked startled and tried to pull himself free. Mr. Bun let go, and the man lost his balance and crashed behind the counter, bringing boxes and cartons down on top of himself.

Mr. Bun closed his eyes. He felt like crying. The thing had suddenly got out of hand. Why hadn't he said he didn't stock the blasted thing and be done with it?

Fearfully, he opened his eyes, and there, amid the broken jars and scattered sweets, sat the man, smiling triumphantly.

'Thees battashots,' he said, waving a bar of something.

'But that's butterscotch,' Mr. Bun protested—then he saw the connection with Laddeeskeert: 'lady's skirt' equalled 'kilt', and butterscotch is, of course, made in Scotland.

The man nodded. 'You no 'ave pundabattashots?'

Mr. Bun drew a deep breath and counted up to ten. 'No, I only sell it in bars.'

'I take two.'

'That'll be twenty pence,' said Mr. Bun, determined not to explode.

When the man had gone, Mr. Bun regarded the mess on the floor, clapped his hat on his head, and went home.

He was grateful to find that his wife had put his dinner in the oven and that it was not ruined.

'You're very quiet tonight,' remarked Mrs. Bun, as she brought in his pudding.

'So would you be if . . .' Mr. Bun stared. 'What's that?'

'Butterscotch caramel cream,' said Mrs. Bun, not at all happy with her husband's tone of voice.

'Well, I'm not eating that, so you know what you can do with it . . .'

And that's how Mr. Bun got his pudding all over his head.

Dopey Ditties

What did they sing when the little dinghy exploded?
Pop Goes the Wee Sail.

What did the baby's parents say?
After the Bawl is Over.

What did the girl say to the hairdresser?
Thank Heaven for Little Curls.

What did they sing after the jousting accident?
All Through the Knight.

What did the devil say when he saw the dangerous roads?
Too Lovely—Black Ice!

What did B say to D?
Oh I Do Like to be Beside the C's Side.

What did the cosy kettle sing?
Home, Home on the Range.

What did the photographer say to the chemist?
Some Day My Prints Will Come.

Factory Fun

'When's tea break?'

'Jenkins accidentally dropped his size ten Wellington boot in.'

'Testing department here . . .'

Animal Jokes

What did the skunk say when the wind changed direction?
'Ah, it's all coming back to me now.'

Did you hear about the two kangaroos who got married?
They lived hoppily ever after.

Shaggy dog story: An Old English sheepdog had her puppies in a rubbish bin because it said: 'PLACE LITTER HERE'.

The new farmhand asked the farmer how long cows should be milked. The farmer replied, 'The same as short ones, of course.'

Advertisement: LION TAMER WANTS TAMER LION.

Mary had a little lamb
Which really was a glutton;
It quickly grew into a sheep
And ended up as mutton.

*'I say, Ferguson,
wouldn't these make wonderful sleeping bags?'*

The Flattered Flying-Fish
by E. V. Rieu

Said the Shark to the Flying-Fish over the phone:
'Will you join me tonight? I am dining alone.
Let me order a nice little dinner for two!
And come as you are, in your shimmering blue.'

Said the Flying-Fish: 'Fancy remembering me,
And the dress that I wore at the Porpoise's tea!'
'How could I forget?' said the Shark in his guile:
'I expect you at eight!' and rang off with a smile.

She has powdered her nose; she has put on her things;
She is off with one flap of her luminous wings.
O little one, lovely, light-hearted and vain,
The Moon will not shine on your beauty again.

Penelope
by Thelwell

The Elephant
by Hilaire Belloc

When people call this beast to mind,
  They marvel more and more

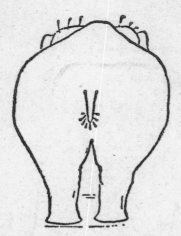

At such a *LITTLE* tail behind

So *LARGE* a trunk before.

More Limericks

There was an Archdeacon who said,
'May I take off my gaiters in bed?'
  But the Bishop said, 'No,
  Wherever you go
You must wear them until you are dead.'

There was an old man of Tralee
Who was bothered to death by a flea,
  So he put out the light,
  Saying, 'Now he can't bite,
For he'll never be able to see.'

A jolly old bear at the Zoo
Could always find something to do.
  When it bored him to go
  On a walk to and fro,
He reversed it, and walked fro and to.

Legs, Eggs, and More Legs

A centipede was happy quite,
Until a frog in fun
Said, 'Pray, which leg comes after which?'
This raised her mind to such a pitch,
She lay distracted in a ditch,
Considering how to run.

The codfish lays ten thousand eggs,
The homely hen lays one.
The codfish never cackles
To tell you what she's done.
And so we scorn the codfish,
While the humble hen we prize,
Which only goes to show you
That it pays to advertise.

You can sing this one to the tune of 'Auld Lang Syne':
On mules we find two legs behind,
And two we find before;
We stand behind before we find
What the two behind be for.
When we're behind the two behind
We find what these be for,
So stand before the two behind,
Behind the two before.

Joking Again

A boy was fishing from the bank of a river when he slipped and fell in. A passer-by pulled him out and asked: 'How did you come to fall in the river?'

'I didn't come to fall in the river,' the boy replied. 'I came to fish.'

Smith: I just saw two policemen chase a hold-up man through a fishmonger's.
Jones: Did they catch him?
Smith: No. He stepped on some scales and got a weigh.

Why does an elephant lie on his back?
To trip low-flying canaries.

Mrs. Smith: I hear your son's in the school football team. What position does he play?
Mrs. Jones: His teacher says he's one of the drawbacks.

A trimmer in a candle factory never worked on Saturdays or Sundays because he was told to take the wick ends off.

Jack: Do you believe in free speech?
Jill: Certainly I do.
Jack: Good! May I use your telephone?

Does an Indian wear feathers to keep his wigwam?

Tommy (saying his prayers): God bless Mum and Dad and make Timbuctoo the capital of Spain.
Mother: Why?
Tommy: Because that's what I put on my examination paper.

'I've always wanted to make a big name for myself.'

'. . . then, after the terrible accident, you'll go down with mumps and then, just as you're getting better . . .'

'Hector—you need a haircut.'

Mr. Bidery's Spidery Garden
by David McCord

Poor old Mr. Bidery.
His garden's awful spidery:
Bugs use it as a hidery.

In April it was seedery,
By May a mess of weedery;
And oh, the bugs! How greedery.

White flowers out or buddery,
Potatoes make it spuddery;
And when it rained, what muddery!

June days grew long and shaddery;
Bullfrog forgets his taddery;
The spider legs his laddery.

MR. BIDERY'S SPIDERY GARDEN

With cabbages so odory,
Snapdragon soon explodery,
At twilight all is toadery.

Young corn still far from foddery,
No sign of goldenrodery,
Yet feeling low and doddery

Is poor old Mr. Bidery,
His garden lush and spidery,
His apples green, not cidery.

Pea-picking *is* so poddery!

More Chuckles

Elsie: Did you meet your son at the station?
Mabel: Oh no, I've known him for years.

Why was the doctor irritable?
Because he had no patients.

She: You remind me of the sea.
He: Wild, romantic and restless?
She: No. You make me sick.

Here's a tale of a Roman galley—a large boat rowed by galley-slaves, who were often beaten to make them row faster.

'I've got some good news and some bad news for you,' said the galley-master to the slaves towards the end of a hard day. 'Which will you have first?'

'The good news,' chorused the exhausted slaves, slumping over their oars.

'Well, the good news is that tonight you will each receive an extra crust of bread.'

'Hooray!' cried the slaves.

'And the bad news,' continued the galley-master, 'is that right now the captain wants to water-ski!'

Father: What station is this? Did they make an announcement?
Son: There was no announcement, Dad. I just heard the porter sneeze.
Father: Ah, then this must be Ashby-de-la-Zouch.

Mad Verse

This is the story of Johnny McGuire,
Who ran through the streets with his trousers on fire.
He went to the doctor's and fainted with fright,
When the doctor told him his end was in sight.

I've got a dog as thin as a rail,
He's got fleas all over his tail;
Every time his tail goes flop,
The fleas at the bottom all jump to the top.

I'm glad the sky is painted blue,
And the earth is painted green,
And such a lot of nice fresh air
Is sandwiched in between.

They strolled the lanes together,
The night was studded with stars;
They reached the gate in silence,
He lifted for her the bars;
She raised her brown eyes to him—
But there's nothing between them now,
For he was only a farmer's boy,
And she was—a Jersey cow.

ible Trouble
Brian White

Answer Me This . . .

Where can you park your car in space?
At a parking meteor.

What did the wig say to the scarf?
'I can see you're all tied up, so I'll go on ahead.'

Why do we say 'Amen' and not 'A women'?
For the same reason that we sing hymns, not hers.

Why is a bachelor a smart fellow?
Because he is never miss-taken.

How should you treat a fat man on board ship?
Give him a wide berth.

Why is a horse very clever?
Because he can eat a meal without a bit in his mouth.

Why did the soldiers cut their tongues out?
Because their boots were too tight.

Why is it bad to write on an empty stomach?
It's not so bad, really, but paper is better.

What's purple and has sixty legs and big teeth?
I don't know, but if you see one—run for your life!

Bird Talk . . .

'Now MARTIN, don't GROUSE. It's SWAN or the other. EIDER you SWALLOW your GOOSEberries or I TERN you out SWIFTly.'

'I GANNET do it. They've still got STORKS on.'

'I KITE aGREBE. Come over RHEA and don't be such a silly COOT, MAVIS. You'll only rEGRET it and TEAL smash the bOWL WREN you're not looking, just for a LARK.'

'Well tHEN, he's a CUCKOO and he gets the BOOBY prize. What a waste of his luncheon VULTURE!'

I Say, I Say, I Say . . .

1st Comic: Robert Burns wrote 'To a Fieldmouse'.
2nd Comic: Did he get an answer?

1st Comic: My girl-friend's a peach.
2nd Comic: You mean she's sweet?
1st Comic: No, she has a heart of stone.

1st Comic: That's a sick-looking watch you've got there.
2nd Comic: Yes. Its hours are numbered.

1st Comic: I'm going to have my appendix out.
2nd Comic: Will you have a scar?
1st Comic: No thanks, I don't smoke.

1st Comic: I'm studying to be a barber.
2nd Comic: Will it take long?
1st Comic: No, I'm learning all the short cuts.

1st Comic: My car's got a puncture.
2nd Comic: How did it happen?
1st Comic: There was a fork in the road.

Daft Definitions

Astronomer: A night watchman

Buttercup: What a goat drinks out of

Copperplate: Policeman's false teeth

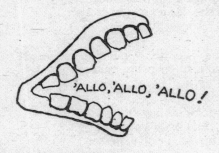

'ALLO, 'ALLO, 'ALLO !

Discover: A record case

Explain: Undecorated eggs

Forceps: A pair of biceps

Garbage: How old your clothes are

Horoscope: A machine for showing horror films

Invest: Protected from the cold

Japonica: Undergarment from Tokyo

Knapsack: A sleeping bag

Lapse: What cats sit on

Modernize: False eyelashes

Neighbourhood: Hat worn by woman next door

Odious: Poetry-loving

Pause: What dogs walk on

Quartermaster: One who teaches fractions

Ringlet: Permission to use the telephone

Skulduggery: Brain surgery

Truant: A real insect

Universe: A short poem

Validate: Fruit found at the bottom of a hill

Warfare: The food soldiers eat

Xmas: Ten mothers

Yule: You will

Zulu: Rest-room in zoological gardens

Batty Boxers

'Three months' hard training, then he has to go and walk into the microphone.'

'When I said show him what you're made of, I didn't mean let him knock the stuffing out of you.'

'Watch out for his right hook . . .'

Even More Limericks

There once was a man who said, 'How
Shall I manage to carry my cow?
   For if I should ask it
   To get in my basket,
'Twould make such a terrible row.'

A housewife called out with a frown,
When surprised by some callers from town,
   'In a minute or less
   I'll slip on a dress——'
But she slipped on the stairs and came down.

The daughter of the farrier
Could find no one to marry her
   Because she said
   She would not wed
A man who could not carry her.

The foolish girl was wrong enough,
And had to wait quite long enough;
   For as she sat
   She grew so fat
That nobody was strong enough!

Crossing Riddles

What do you get if you cross:

A chirping insect with a flying mouse?
A cricket bat.

A blast of wind with a mathematician?
A puff adder.

A library with a maggot?
A bookworm.

A sneeze with a news sheet?
Tissue paper.

A porcupine with a goat?
A stuck-up kid.

A freezer with a bank?
An ice lolly.

A tropical fruit with a white stick?
A blind date.

A tape measure with a steamroller?
Flat feet.

Our Friend Augustus
and his Faithful Hound
by A. S. Graham

'And that, sir, is I believe the card you originally
thought of . . .'

'Oh, good! Still half an hour to go . . .'

The Cannibal Chief

Okee-Pokee-Crack-me-Crown,
King of the Island of Gulp-em-down,
Was thought the finest young fellow in town
When dressed in his best for a party.

Oka-Poka-Chinga-ma-ring,
Eighteenth wife of this mighty king,
Loved her lord above everything,
And dressed him out for the party.

Satins and silks the queen did lack,
But she'd some red paint that looked well on black,
So she painted her lord and master's back
Before he went out to the party.

Crowns and stars, and ships with sails,
And flying dragons with curly tails—
'That's a dress,' said the queen, 'that never fails
To charm all folks at a party.'

So, painted up till he looked his best,
With pipe in mouth and feather in crest,
Okee-Pokee marched out without coat or vest,
But yet in full dress, to the party.

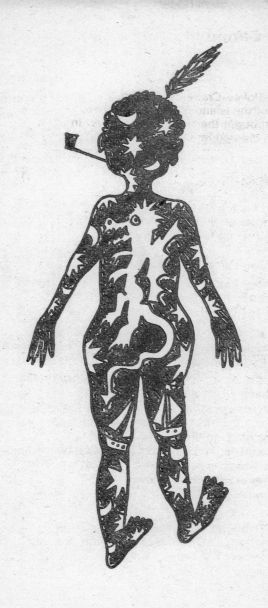

Just Jokes

Teacher: Annie, can you tell me what happens when a body is immersed in liquid?
Annie: The phone rings.

A man had a dream in which he saw the number 7 above a race course. The next day he put £7 on horse number 7 in the 7th race. It came 7th.

Don: My budgie weighs 14 stone.
Ron: What do you call him?
Don: Sir.

Liverpool Lad (in a furrier's shop): I'd like to buy a coat.
Assistant: What fur?
Liverpool Lad: Fur me girlfriend.

Did you hear about the man who ran over himself? He asked me to pop across the street and buy some cigarettes. I wouldn't go, so he ran over himself.

Roadsweeper: I'm fed up with this job, guv. It's brush this road, brush that road, all day long. I've got too many roads to brush.
Foreman: Right. I'll see to it that tomorrow you only have two roads to brush.
Roadsweeper: Great! Which roads?
Foreman: The M1 and the M6.

Lady Traveller: Can you give me a room and a bath?
Hotel Clerk: I can give you a room, but you'll have to give yourself a bath.

Crazy Creatures

If you should meet a crocodile,
Don't take a stick and poke him;
Ignore the welcome in his smile,
Be careful not to stroke him.
For as he sleeps upon the Nile,
He thinner gets and thinner;
And whene'er you meet a crocodile
He's ready for his dinner.

What a strange bird the frog are.
When he sit he stand almost;
When he jump he fly almost;
When he talk he cry almost;
He ain't got no sense hardly.
He ain't got no tail hardly, either.
He sit on what he ain't got almost.

Ooey Gooey was a worm,
A little worm was he.
He sat upon the railroad tracks,
The train he did not see.
Ooey Gooey!

Cat-astrophes

Catacomb

Caterwaul

Caterpillar

Catalogue

Kids' Stuff

'Hello, and here's a list of things I won't eat.'

'It's a pretty poor sort of father who won't cut himself to please his own daughter.'

'They asked me if I was interested in trains, and I fell for it!'

What the Wiggle-Woggle Said
by Spike Milligan

The Wiggle-Woggle said,
'I wish that I were dead:
I've a pain in my tummy and
It's travelling up the bed.
I wish that I were something
That never got a pain;
A little bit of fluffy stuff
That vanished down the drain.
I could be a tiger's whisker,
A tuba made of bread,
The purple eye
Of a custard pie
With a trouser made of lead.
There *must* be other somethings—
A tiny leather bead?
Or a bit of crumpled paper
Where the water-melons feed?
A yellow thing with lumps on!
A yellow thing without!!
Some hairy stuff
On a powder puff
That snuffs the candles out.
Wish i were a lamp post
(Lamp posts don't get pains),
A leaky rusty gutter
Flooding other people's drains!
All *those* are what I'd like to be,'
The Wiggle-Woggle said.

But he stayed a Wiggle-Woggle
And, what's more, he stayed in bed!

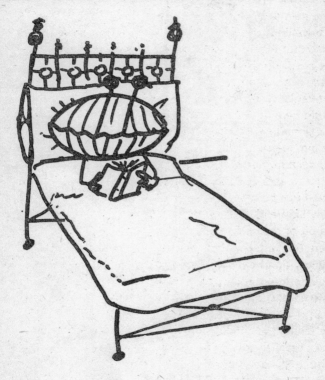

Gallery Giggles

THE DYING ITALIAN
BY
KIKA D. BUCKET

'Winged Dinosaur' by Terry Dacktill

'Angel Choirs' by Hal E. Looyah

'A Summer Garden' by Petunia Bed

'The Good Samaritan' by Ada Stranger

'Niagara Sunset' by Walter Fall

'Jungle Giants' by L. E. Fant

'Breakfast Table' by M. N. Eggs

'The English Gentleman' by Steve Upperlip

'Motorway Transport' by Laurie Lode

GALLERY GIGGLES

'An Old Church' by Norman Arch

'The First Noel' by Carol Singer

'The Gull' by A. C. Bird

'Brigade of Guards' by Reggie Ment

'The Advertisement' by Bill Sticker

'Grey Skies' by Ann T. Cyclone

'Intersecting Lines' by Chris Cross

'Signpost' by Hugo Yorway

'The Weekend Bride' by Marion Sunday

'Vegetable Plot' by Carl E. Flower

'The Apache Warrior' by Tom A. Hawk

'Bleeding Hearts' by Val N. Tine

'Chinese Boat' by Sam Pan

'Fiery Devils' by Helen Damnation

'Sweet Afton' by Flo Gently

'The Barmaid' by Phyllis Glassup

'A Funeral' by Diane B. Buried

'Charging Bull' by Esau Redd

'Back From Holiday' by Geoff A. Nicetime

Hayseeds
by Hargreaves

Limerick Ladies

There was a young lady of Harwich,
Who behaved very bad at her marwich,
   She proceeded on skates
   To the parish church gates,
While her friends followed on in the carwich.

There was an old lady of Leith,
Who had most remarkable teeth;
   They were not very strong,
   But so spiky and long
That she had to keep each in a sheath!

There was an old lady of Harrow
Who rode a large hamster to Jarrow,
   Where they swam in the sea
   And ate fishcakes for tea;
Then she wheeled him home in a barrow.

Edward Lear's Nonsense Botany

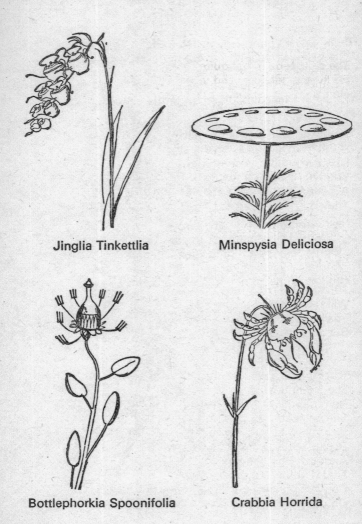

Jinglia Tinkettlia

Minspysia Deliciosa

Bottlephorkia Spoonifolia

Crabbia Horrida

The Centipede
by A. P. Herbert

The centipede is not quite nice;
He lives in idleness and vice;
He has a hundred legs.
He also has a hundred wives,
And each of these if she survives
Has just a hundred eggs;
So that's the reason if you pick
Up any boulder, stone or brick
You nearly always find
A swarm of centipedes concealed;
They scatter far across the field,
But *one* remains behind.
And you may reckon then, my son,
That not alone that luckless one
Lies pitiful and torn,
But millions more of either sex—
100 multiplied by X—
Will never now be born;
I dare say it will make you sick,
But so does all Arithmetic.

The gardener says, I ought to add,
The centipede is not so bad;
He rather likes the brutes.
The millipede is what he loathes;
He uses wild bucolic oaths
Because it eats his roots;
And every gardener is agreed
That if you see a centipede
Conversing with a milli—
On one of them you drop a stone,

111

THE CENTIPEDE

The other one you leave alone—
I think that's rather silly;
They may be right, but what I say
Is 'Can one stand about all day
And *count* the creatures legs?'
It has too many any way,
And any moment it may lay
Another hundred eggs!
So if I see a thing like *this*

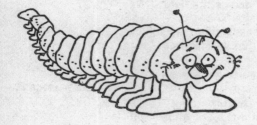

I murmur 'Without prejudice,'
And knock it on the head;
And if I see a thing like *that*

I take a brick and squash it flat;
In either case, it's dead.

Kids!

Mother: Did you take a bath today, Harry?
Harry: Why? Is there one missing?

A ten-year-old boy was smoking a cigarette when a man came up to him and said, 'Aren't you a bit young for that?'

'Oh no,' said the boy. 'I go out with girls, as well. I was out with one last night, as a matter of fact.'

The man frowned. 'And how old was she?'

'Blowed if I know,' replied the boy. 'I was too drunk to ask her.'

Helen: Let's play school.
Ellen: O.K. But let's play I'm absent.

Why are little boys like flannel?
Because they shrink from washing.

Old Lady: Are you a good boy, then?
Jimmy: Nope. I'm the kind of boy my mother doesn't want me to play with.

*'You haven't heard the worst yet—
there's going to be a silver collection.'*

Barkers

'You're spoiling
that dog, Joe.

Nonsense Riddles

Where are happy marriages made?
Gretna Grin.

Where do they make laws with holes in them?
The Houses of Peppermint.

What did the budgie become after the lawn-mower ran over it?
Shredded tweet.

Who was the cleanest President of the United States?
George Washingmachine.

What has long hair and weighs two tons?
A hippiepotamus.

Which Italian statesman had no hair?
Gary Baldy.

Who was the first prehistoric novelist?
Charlotte Brontesaurus.

Who wrote 'Alice Through the Cabbage Patch'?
Lewis Carrot.

Who had a corn as high as an elephant's eye?
Oscar Hammertoes.

As They Say . . .

Striking a light

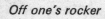

Off one's rocker

Raising the alarm

116

Catching fire

No time at all

Coming to terms

An Odd Fellow

from 'The Hunting of the Snark' **by Lewis Carroll**

There was one who was famed for the number of things
   He forgot when he entered the ship:
His umbrella, his watch, all his jewels and rings,
   And the clothes he had bought for the trip.

He had forty-two boxes, all carefully packed,
   With his name painted clearly on each;
But, since he omitted to mention the fact,
   They were all left behind on the beach.

The loss of his clothes hardly mattered, because
   He had seven coats on when he came,
With three pairs of boots—but the worst of it was,
   He had wholly forgotten his name.

He would answer to 'Hi!' or to any loud cry,
   Such as 'Fry me!' or 'Fritter my wig!'
To 'What-you-may-call-um!' or 'What-was-his-name!'
   But especially 'Thing-um-a-jig!'

While, for those who preferred a more forcible word,
   He had different names from these:
His intimate friends called him 'Candle-ends',
   And his enemies 'Toasted-cheese'.

Sad Endings

Here lies what's left of William Dough—
With us he is no more,
For what he thought was H_2O
Was H_2SO_4.

There was an old woman, her name it was Peg;
Her head was of wood. and she wore a cork leg.
Her neighbours all pitched her into the water.
Her leg was drowned first, and her head followed after.

Willie saw some dynamite;
Couldn't understand it quite.
Curiosity never pays.
It rained Willie seven days!

He rocked the boat,
Did Ezra Shank;
These bubbles

        o
         o
       o
     o
    o
   o
  o
     mark
Where Ezra sank.

What? More Limericks?

There was a young fellow named Clyde;
Who once at a funeral was spied;
When asked who was dead,
He smilingly said,
'I don't know—I just came for the ride!'

A cannibal chief of Penzance
Ate an uncle and two of his aunts,
And then a large piece
Of a rather fat niece,
And now he can't button his pants.

I'd rather have fingers than toes;
I'd rather have ears than a nose;
And as for my hair,
I'm glad that it's there.
I'll be awfully sad when it goes.

Ho! Ho!

Teacher: Today we will talk about the heart, liver and kidneys.
Pupil: Oh dear, another organ recital.

Did you hear about the astronomer? He was starry-eyed because his business was looking up.

Freddy: I dropped my watch in the Thames three years ago and it's still running.
Neddy: The same watch?
Freddy: No, the Thames.

A young lady had an accident in her car.
   'Now then,' said a policeman, pulling out his notebook, 'what gear were you in when you approached the cross-roads?'
   'Same as now,' replied the young lady. 'Green dress, red belt and black shoes.'

'Dear o£d Dad: How are you and a££ the fami£y? You wi££ be p£eased to hear I am doing we££ at schoo£. £ots of £ove, Bi££.'
'Dear Bill: It's good to kNOw that NOthing's wrong. Write us aNOther letter soon. Must go NOw. See you aNOn. Love, Dad.'

Three men fell into the water, but only two got their hair wet.
Why? One of them was bald.

The Butler
by Archibald Marshall

When Mr. and Mrs. Gumble got rich they thought they would like a butler because it was grander, so they put it in the newspaper that they would give a kind home to a really good butler and pay him plenty of wages. And the one they chose was called Hicks, and they chose him because he had been butler to an Earl before, and they didn't know any Earls yet but they wanted to know some, and they thought perhaps Hicks might introduce them to his Earl. And when they asked him he said well perhaps I might if I am satisfied with the place, but you must do everything I tell you because you are both very common indeed.

And Mr. Gumble said well I know we are, but I suppose we can improve if we try.

And the butler said oh yes, but you will never be anything much because you haven't begun soon enough, still you can be better than you are, and of course people won't mind you being a little common because you are so rich.

So he told Mr. and Mrs. Gumble how to behave properly, and they got on pretty well with it because they tried hard and only had a holiday sometimes when they were alone.

And then Mr. Gumble said do you think you could introduce us to the Earl now, we have got on so well that I'm sure we shouldn't offend him, and if he would come and have dinner with us we could put it in the newspaper next day and everybody would see how we are getting on.

So the butler went to the Earl and he said look here will you come and have dinner with Mr. and Mrs. Gumble,

123

they are rather common but they are very rich and it might be a good thing for you.

And the Earl said well how much will they pay me for it, because I want some more money and it would be one way of getting it.

And the butler said well they might be rather shocked if an Earl wanted to be paid for having dinner with them, but I'll tell you what, after dinner you could ask Mr. Gumble if he would lend you some money, and then you could forget to pay him back.

So the Earl said oh very well, and he went and had dinner with Mr. and Mrs. Gumble, and he was very polite to them and told them about Queen Victoria and King Edward, and Mrs. Gumble said to him well I had no idea that Earls were so nice and I wish I knew some more of them.

And the butler was pouring out some wine, and he said well perhaps you will if you go on learning how to behave, you have done pretty well this evening but now it is time you went away, because gentlemen don't want ladies with them when they are talking together after dinner, of course you are not really a lady but it's all the same.

And Mrs. Gumble said oh I didn't know, ought I to go to bed now or go and sit in the drawing-room?

And the butler said you had better go and sit in the drawing-room, and when the gentlemen have drunk enough wine they will go there too.

And the Earl said oh I'm afraid I can't do that because I promised some other Earls to go and play at cards with them when I had had enough dinner.

And the butler said to Mr. Gumble yes you can't expect him to stay here all evening when you are so common, I wonder he has stayed so long.

And Mr. Gumble said well I suppose he wanted to finish his dinner, and Mrs. Gumble said to the Earl well thank you very much for coming, and I am sorry we are so common but we can't help it because we were born like that. And she went away and sat in the drawing-room on a sofa, and she took off her shoes because they were so tight.

Well directly they were left alone together the Earl said to Mr. Gumble do you think you could lend me some money, because I have got a lot of things to pay for and I haven't got enough.

And Mr. Gumble said how much money? And he said the more the better.

So Mr. Gumble said well I might, but when will you be able to pay me back?

And the Earl said oh I don't know, I will some day.

And Mr. Gumble said well I will lend you half a crown, and he took one out of his pocket and put it on the table.

Well the Earl was rather disappointed because he had thought of something more like a thousand pounds, but he took the half-crown and said thank you, and then he said well I'm afraid I can't stay any longer, but I haven't drunk quite enough wine yet, would you mind if I took the rest of the bottle away with me?

And Mr. Gumble said no I don't mind, I have got plenty more bottles of wine downstairs, but I didn't know Earls did that.

And the Earl said well some do and some don't, would you mind ringing the bell for the butler? I would do it myself but I am a little tipsy, and when I am like that I can't walk quite straight.

So Mr. Gumble rang the bell and the butler came, and the Earl said to him order Mr. Gumble's motor-car please to take me away, I have had enough of this and he has only lent me half a crown so it isn't worth while stopping any longer.

So the butler ordered the motor-car, and he and the chauffeur carried the Earl down to it with the rest of the bottle of wine and he went away.

Well after some time Mr. Gumble said to the butler I think it is time the Earl paid me back my half-crown, and you had better go and ask him for it.

And the butler looked at the ceiling and he said oh how common to ask an Earl to pay you back half a crown, I don't think I shall ever be able to do anything with you, you get worse and worse every day.

And Mr. Gumble said I don't care whether I do or not, I am going to have my half-crown back or I shall have the Earl sent to prison, and he has got a decanter of mine which he has never sent back either, I don't mind him having the wine that was in it but I am not going to let him keep the decanter.

So the butler had to go to the Earl, and the Earl said well you can have the decanter but I can't give you the half-crown because I spent it long ago.

And the butler said well Mr. Gumble will have you sent to prison if you don't.

So the Earl said oh well then I shall have to sell my wife's diamond tiara, I was afraid it would come to that but it can't be helped, perhaps Mr. Gumble would like to buy it for Mrs. Gumble, you might ask him.

Well of course Mr. Gumble could easily have afforded to buy his wife several diamond tiaras if he had wanted to, but he hadn't thought of it before, and he bought the Earl's wife's tiara fairly cheap and Mrs. Gumble went to the opera with it. And everybody said how grand she was, and a lot of people thought it would be a good thing to get to know the Gumbles because they seemed so rich.

So after that Mr. and Mrs. Gumble got on very well and they weren't quite so common as they had been because of the butler telling them how not to be. And the butler said you must pay me double wages now, because it is all through me that you have got on so well.

And Mr. Gumble said I won't pay you double wages,

but I'll tell you what I will do, I will give you the sack. And the butler said what for?

And he said why for keeping on calling me and Mrs. Gumble common I have had enough of it.

And the butler said well I do call that unfair, and Mr. Gumble said I don't care whether you do or not, we have got on so well now that we can do without you.

So the butler had to go and the Earl had spent all his money by this time, so they set up a fishmonger's shop between them, and Mrs. Gumble always bought her fish from them because she was sorry for the Earl and she rather liked the butler, but she told them not to tell Mr. Gumble.